Learn The Skill Of Exploring In A Negotiation

How To Develop The Skill Of Exploring What Is Possible In A Negotiation In Order To Reach The Best Possible Deal

"Practical, proven techniques that will help you get the best deal possible out of your next negotiation"

Dr. Jim Anderson

Published by:
Blue Elephant Consulting
Tampa, Florida

Copyright © 2013 by Dr. Jim Anderson

All rights reserved. No part of this book may be reproduced of transmitted in any form or by any means, electronic or mechanical, including photocopying, recording or by any information storage and retrieval system without written permission of the publisher, except for inclusion of brief quotations in a review.

Printed in the United States of America

Library of Congress Control Number: 2013957209

ISBN-13: 978-1494426880

ISBN-10: 1494426889

Warning – Disclaimer

The purpose of this book is to educate and entertain. This book does not promise or guarantee that anyone following the ideas, tips, suggestions, techniques or strategies will be successful. The author, publisher and distributor(s) shall have neither liability nor responsibility to anyone with respect to any loss or damage caused, or alleged to be caused, directly or indirectly by the information contained in this book.

Recent Books By The Author

Product Management

- Product Development Lessons For Product Managers: How Product Managers Can Create Successful Products

- Customer Lessons For Product Managers: Techniques For Product Managers To Better Understand What Their Customers Really Want

Public Speaking

- How To Give A Great Presentation: Presentation techniques that will transform a speech into a memorable event

- How To Rehearse In Order To Give The Perfect Speech: How to effectively rehearse your next speech to that your message be remembered forever!

CIO Skills

- Critical CIO Management Skills: Decision Making Skills That Every CIO Needs To Have In Order To Be Able To Make The Right Choices

- How CIOs Can Make Innovation Happen: Tips And Techniques For CIOs To Use In Order To Make Innovation Happen In Their IT Department

IT Manager Skills

- Staffing Skills IT Managers Must Have: Tips And Techniques That IT Managers Can Use In Order To Correctly Staff Their Teams

- Secrets Of Effective Leadership For IT Managers: Tips And Techniques That IT Managers Can Use In Order To Develop Leadership Skills

Negotiating

- Learn How To Argue In Your Next Negotiation: How To Develop The Skill Of Effective Arguing In A Negotiation In Order To Get The Best Possible Outcome

- How To Open Your Next Negotiation: How To Start A Negotiation In Order To Get The Best Possible Outcome

Miscellaneous

- Power Distribution Unit (PDU) Secrets: What Everyone Who Works In A Data Center Needs To Know!

- Making The Jump: How To Land Your Dream Job When You Get Out Of College!

Note: See a complete list of books by Dr. Jim Anderson at the back of this book.

Acknowledgements

Any book like this one is the result of years of real-world work experience. In my over 25 years of working for 7 different firms, I have met countless fantastic people and I've been mentored by some truly exceptional ones. Although I've probably forgotten some of the people who made me the person that I am today, here is my attempt to finally give them the recognition that they so truly deserve:

- Thomas P. Anderson
- Art Puett
- Bobbi Marshall
- Bob Boggs

Dr. Jim Anderson

This book is dedicated to my wife Lori. None of this would have been possible without her love and support.

Thanks for the best 21 years of my life (so far)...!

Table Of Contents

THE DEAL THAT YOU WANT CAN ONLY BE FOUND BY EXPLORING.....8

ABOUT THE AUTHOR 10

CHAPTER 1: GOT TO KEEP 'EM SEPARATED — ROLES IN NEGOTIATING 15

CHAPTER 2: MICROSOFT / YAHOO — WHEN NEGOTIATIONS GO BAD 18

CHAPTER 3: YOU WANT A BARGAIN? LEARN HOW OTHER CULTURES BARTER 21

CHAPTER 4: FUNNY MONEY AIN'T SO FUNNY WHEN IT'S YOUR MONEY 24

CHAPTER 5: EVEN THE EXPERTS SCREW UP: 7 YEARS OF WASTED NEGOTIATIONS 27

CHAPTER 6: THE JAMES BOND APPROACH TO NEGOTIATING 30

CHAPTER 7: TESTING THE WATERS: DOES THE OTHER SIDE REALLY MEAN THAT?...33

CHAPTER 8: IT'S KRUNCH TIME! 36

CHAPTER 9: DO YOU MIND IF I "NIBBLE" ON YOU?.........................39

CHAPTER 10: HOW DO YOU DEAL WITH THE REST OF THE ICEBERG DURING A NEGOTIATION?..43

CHAPTER 11: WHAT IF THERE WAS NO "WHAT IF" NEGOTIATION TACTIC?...47

CHAPTER 12: NEGOTIATION TACTIC: THE REVERSE AUCTION...........50

The Deal That You Want Can Only Be Found By Exploring

When you start a negotiation, there is a great deal that you don't know. No matter how much homework and research that you've done in order to better understand the other side of the table and their position, there will always be things that you don't know.

This means that there will be a great deal that you will have to learn while the negotiation is going on. In order for this to happen, you are going to have to master the skill of exploring what is possible during the negotiation.

Your goal during the negotiation has to be to use your exploring skills to seek understanding and possibility. You'll never know what the other side is going to be willing to agree to until you ask them.

A key part of developing your negotiating exploring skills is to understand the different roles in every negotiation. Who has what roles may be influenced by the different cultures that are involved in your negotiations.

If you don't take the time to fully explore what is possible in your negotiation, then you may not be able to reach a deal with the other side. All too often in today's business environment we read about major deals falling apart. We need to study these events and understand why they happened and how we can avoid a similar fate.

There are vast arrays of negotiating tools that are available to you in order to assist you with your exploring. With exotic sounding names such as the "krunch" tactic, "nibbling", and even the "reverse auction" each of these exploring tools is available for you to use in order to get the best deal possible.

This book has been written to provide you with a complete overview of what the negotiating skill of exploring is. We'll be taking a look at the benefits of exploring, the tactics used, and what kind of results you can expect. Read the book and you'll become a more skilled negotiator!

For more information on what it takes to be a great negotiator, check out my blog, The Accidental Negotiator, at:

www.TheAccidentalNegotiator.com

Good luck!

- Dr. Jim Anderson

About The Author

I must confess that I never set out to be a negotiator. When I went to school, I studied Computer Science and thought that I'd get a nice job programming and that would be that. Well, at least part of that plan worked out!

My first job was working for Boeing on their F/A-18 fighter jet program. I spent my days programming fighter jet software in assembly language and I loved it. The U.S. government decided to save some money and went looking for other countries to sell this plane to. This put me into an unfamiliar role: I started to negotiate with foreign military officials and I ended up having to participate in the negotiations for large international deals.

Time moved on and so did I. I found myself working for Siemens, the big German telecommunications company. They were making phone switches and selling them to the seven U.S. phone companies. The problem was that the switches were too complicated. When it came time to negotiate a deal with the customer, the sales teams struggled to create an effective negotiating strategy. I was called in to bridge the world between the product functionality and the business impacts as they related to the negotiations.

I've spent over 25 years working as a negotiator for both big companies and startups. This has given me an opportunity to learn what it takes to both plan and execute negotiations of all sizes. When it comes to negotiations, I've pretty much been there, done that.

I now live in Tampa Florida where I spend my time managing my consulting business, Blue Elephant Consulting, teaching college courses at the University of South Florida, and traveling to work with companies like yours to share the knowledge that I have about how to prepare for and execute successful negotiations.

I'm always available to answer questions and I can be reached at:

Dr. Jim Anderson
Blue Elephant Consulting
Email: jim@BlueElephantConsulting.com
Facebook: http://goo.gl/1TVoK
Web: **www.BlueElephantConsulting.com**

"Unforgettable communication skills that will set your ideas free..."

Create An Effective Negotiating Team At Your Company!

Dr. Jim Anderson is available to provide training and coaching on the topics that are the most important to people who have to negotiate: how can my team effectively prepare for and execute a successful negotiation that will get us what we both want and need?

Dr. Anderson believes that in order to both learn and remember what he says, audiences need to laugh. Each one of his speeches is full of fun and humor so that what he says "sticks" with everyone.

Dr. Anderson's Negotiating Training Includes:

1. How to plan for a negotiation: what information do you need and where can you find it?

2. What's the best way to explore how a deal can be created during a negotiation?

3. How can you bring a negotiation to a close without giving in to the other side?

Dr. Jim Anderson works with over 100 customers per year. To invite Dr. Anderson to work with you, contact him at:

Phone: 813-418-6970 or
Email: jim@BlueElephantConsulting.com

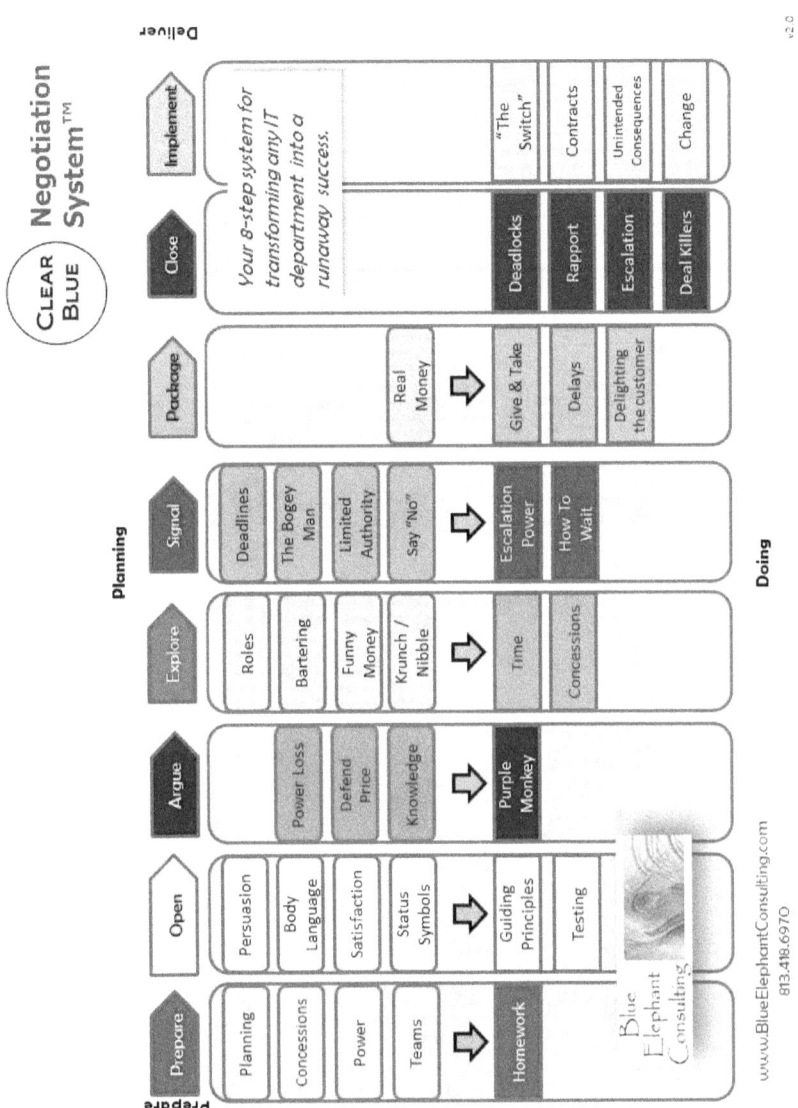

The **Clear Blue Negotiation System™** has been created to provide negotiators with a clear roadmap for how to manage a successful negotiation. This system shows negotiators what needs to be done and in what order to do it.

Chapter 1

Got To Keep 'Em Separated — Roles In Negotiating

Chapter 1: Got To Keep 'Em Separated — Roles In Negotiating

It really doesn't matter if you are negotiating to buy a car, buy a house, buy a new email system for your company, or just where you and your significant other will go out to dinner on Friday night. In every negotiating situation, you need to realize that there are different roles to be played and they need to be kept separate.

If you are a team of one doing the negotiating, then you need to keep this in mind and switch roles as needed. What are the roles you ask? Why that's simple:

1. **The Commander**: this is the person who makes the final decisions. At work this may be your boss. In a negotiation, this is the person who needs to sign off on your side of the deal. If you are buying a car, this may be your significant other who you have to run the deal by to get final approval.

2. **The Negotiator**: this is the person who does most of the talking. The negotiator does not have the authority to make final decisions; however, he/she is the one who puts the deal together by talking with the other side. The relationship that the other side forms with the negotiator is the key to determining how the negotiations go.

3. **The Scribe**: this is the person who takes down notes throughout the negotiations. Negotiations can stretch on for hours/days/months. It can be very difficult to remember what was agreed to or what was said in the past hour or day or month. The scribe takes careful notes and makes sure that the negotiator can easily find

the information that they need.

4. **The Floater**: Negotiations always require more information than is currently available. The floater is the person who gets things, checks things, and confirms things. The floaters' activities are designed to allow the negotiator to focus on the negotiations without having to constantly go searching for additional material.

Needless to say, all too often we find ourselves playing all four roles. Just be aware that you are playing these separate roles and make sure that the other side knows this too.

This way when the other side starts to pressure your negotiator role to agree to something, you can push back by saying "I need some time to think about this." In this way you can buy your Commander role some time to make a good decision.

Chapter 2

Microsoft / Yahoo — When Negotiations Go Bad

Chapter 2: Microsoft / Yahoo — When Negotiations Go Bad

It happened a while ago, but Microsoft tried to buy Yahoo. However, Microsoft's offer to buy Yahoo fell through. What's interesting about this from a negotiator point-of-view is that it offers a number of important lessons for us mere mortals who only occasionally get to practice negotiating.

First we need to set the stage. According to Yahoo sources, here's how things went:

- Microsoft showed up with a $31/share offer to buy Yahoo.

- Yahoo said no thanks — we're worth $40/share.

- Microsoft stayed fixed at $31.

- Yahoo came back at $38.

- Microsoft stayed firm at $31.

- Yahoo came back at $37.

- Microsoft came up to $33

- Yahoo would not budge at $37

- Microsoft walked away.

Nothing is ever this simple, but price was clearly one of the key sticking points of the negotiations. This tells us that at $37/share, Microsoft decided that their BATNA (Best Alternative To A Negotiated Agreement) was better. What is not quite so clear is that there were a number of handicaps that were restricting the negotiations for both sides:

- Steve Ballmer (Microsoft) could still follow through on his threat to do away with formalities and circumvent the Yahoo board with the promised proxy tactic.

- Microsoft has to make sure to keep its behavior in check throughout this process lest its image as a monopoly that crushes everything in its path be confirmed.

- Yahoo has to be careful that its shareholders not be left with the feeling that because of a Jerry Yang/Steve Ballmer personality conflict they were robbed of a significant payback on their investment in Yahoo stock.

- Yahoo has to think about their employees — since there is such a us vs. them mentality when it comes to Microsoft, what would happen if Microsoft did buy Yahoo — would any of that valuable intellectual property be left?

Nothing is ever as it seems and clearly both sides did not do all of the homework that was required before starting these negotiations.

If they had, the discussions would have been done at the negotiating table and not in the flurry of press releases that were issued while the talks dragged on. Oh well, their loss is full of lessons for all of us.

Chapter 3

You Want A Bargain? Learn How Other Cultures Barter

Chapter 3: You Want A Bargain? Learn How Other Cultures Barter

Although we pride ourselves on living in modern times, the art of negotiating is an ancient skill that our relatives who lived in more humble times probably did better than we do. Don't despair — there's no need to feel like a dummy! What your ancestors once knew can be quickly relearned

There are three negotiating skills that your grandfather's grandfather used every time he ventured to market:

1. **Always leave yourself room to negotiate (& grant concessions)**: When trying to buy something, consider the price that is advertised for anything as simply a starting point no matter if it's vegetables in the market or a giant wide-screen TV.

   Whatever you first propose as a price that you'd be willing to pay, make sure that the gap between it and the advertised price is great enough that you've got plenty of room left with to negotiate in. The flip side to this rule is that your starting price needs to be high enough so that it does not appear to be insulting.

2. **Concede Slowly**: In every negotiation, you will end up giving some things away — that is the very nature of negotiations. What's really important is how fast you give it away! The slower you are to give in on various points, the more time you'll have to get what you want out of the negotiations.

3. **Ask For Something In Return When You Make A Concession**: As silly as it sounds, this is actually very

important. If when you make a concession you don't ask for something, then the other side is going to end up feeling dissatisfied.

They are going to feel as though it was too easy for you to give up what you offered. So instead, make sure that every agreement that the other side drags out of you has something that you get from them. Once again note that what you get does not have to have an equivalent value.

There you go! Armed with these three trusty guides you are once again ready to do your family proud the next time you venture to the market.

Chapter 4

Funny Money Ain't So Funny When It's YOUR Money

Chapter 4: Funny Money Ain't So Funny When It's YOUR Money

In the world of negotiating we spend a lot of time talking about "funny money". You should know what it is because it can end up costing you a lot of real money even if you don't think that you made any concessions during the negotiation!

We all know what "real" money is – we can touch it, we can spend it, and we know how much of it we have. Funny money is exactly the opposite of this: taxes, credit cards, monthly payments, and interest rates all fall into this category of funny money.

Watch any car commercial on TV and you'll see that car dealers learned a long time ago that it is much easier to sell a car as "$300 a month" instead of a very scary $40,000. The subprime mortgage mess is yet another example of the same thing: even if you really can't afford a $200,000 house, maybe you can afford $500 a month until interest rates go up.

A few examples of how funny money sneaks its way into negotiations include:

- Dollars per hour

- A five year warranty

- "Points" (percentage points on a deal, often found in real estate deals)

- Price w/o delivery

- A 5% fee.

- Monthly payments

In the end, the key thing to remember about funny money when you are negotiating is that you should never negotiate for or about funny money unless you have spent the time BEFORE negotiating to think things through completely.

Funny money may not really exist; however, you know what real money is and you can lose a lot of that if you don't watch what is happening with the funny money!

Chapter 5

Even The Experts Screw Up: 7 Years Of Wasted Negotiations

Chapter 5: Even The Experts Screw Up: 7 Years Of Wasted Negotiations

What would you expect the very best negotiators in the world would spend their time doing? Whatever it was, it would have to have something to do with money and lots of it. We're probably talking about billions and billions here.

Well guess what, a whole bunch of them work for the World Trade Organization (WTO) which is located in Geneva and they just screwed up big time: a 7-year effort to forge a new global trade pact collapsed a while ago. There now – don't you feel better about your negotiating abilities?

First Microsoft and Yahoo couldn't find a way to make a deal and now this. What happened and why couldn't the big boys resolve this issue?

In a nutshell, the negotiations had dragged on for so long that the priorities of the 30 or so players involved had changed. Specifically, what was being negotiated was for developing countries such as China and India to lower their tariffs on industrial goods from the West while the West would cut tariff and subsidy's on farm products.

Sounds simple enough, doesn't it? What caused this train to come off its tracks was that the developing countries wanted the ability to raise tariffs on imports if there was a sudden surge in imports.

The big deal was not if this could be done, but rather how best to define a "surge". China and India wanted to set the trigger at 10%, the U.S. wanted to set it at 40%. Neither side could agree, and so now the whole deal is off.

So what really happened here students of the negotiating arts? Clearly both sides of this deal felt that they had a better option than the one that was on the table.

The experts say that individual countries will now go on negotiating bilateral trade deals. However, one downside to this is that the WTO may now be seen as being weaker and may be less able to help resolve issues that show up in existing agreements.

What can we eager learners learn from all of this? Two things: you should always make sure that you research and fully understand what the other side's alternatives are. This will help you to better understand just how firm you can stand on a given issue during the negotiations.

Secondly, you must realize that the more parties that are involved in the negotiations, the longer and more drawn out the negotiations will be. Do your research and only negotiate at a short table and maybe you'll be able to complete your next negotiation in less than 7 years and with better results!

Chapter 6

The James Bond Approach To Negotiating

Chapter 6: The James Bond Approach To Negotiating

The other day I happened to drop in on my friend Mike only to discover him hard at work on some mysterious project. He had a list of local electronics stores and he was checking them off with a pencil one-by-one.

All the while he was surfing a seemingly endless set of web sites and performing a cut and paste operation from each one of them to an Excel spreadsheet that already looked like a day trader's tracking system.

When I asked him what he was up to, he told me that he had finally broken down and was going to buy the Panasonic 50" TV of his dreams. His plan was to buy it that evening.

He wanted to buy it at the Best Buy located close to his house so that he could get it home and start watching it that night. When I inquired as to why all of the frantic action was taking place, he just stared at me for a moment and said *"...if I want to get the best price, then I've got to do some espionage to find out how low they can go..."*

Ok, so I guess that I should have seen that one coming. Mike did bring up a very good point: often the outcome of a negotiation is determined before the talking even starts and the winner is the side that collected the BEST information.

Note that I didn't say the MOST information, because this is a case where quality definitely triumphs over quantity. Getting more information on the other person's situation, constraints, and motivations will increase your power while allowing you to do a better job of defending your important issues.

You can't view information gathering as a one-shot activity. It is a process that continues even after the negotiations start and that will require you to shift in and out of multiple modes during the negotiations.

You should look at information gathering as a process that will continue throughout the entire negotiation session. This means that you'll need to establish a personal connection with the other side before you jump into the heart of your negotiation. The ability to see and understand the other side's viewpoint is critical to understanding their negotiating position.

In business to business negotiations one of the most often overlooked sources of information is your staff no matter what department they are in. Often times we have employees who used to work for the other side, or employees who have close personal connections to the other side's staff. These are great resources to draw on in order to learn more about the set of environmental drivers that will be shaping the other side's negotiating position.

I gave Mike a call yesterday in order to find out how his purchase had turned out. He was beside himself with glee. *"When they saw me come in with my stack of research papers, they turned me over to the manager right away. He and I talked for about 45 minutes and in the end I had gotten $400 off of the list price and a free 1 year warranty."* It looks like you can put a price tag on the value of gathering information.

Chapter 7

Testing The Waters: Does The Other Side Really Mean That?

Chapter 7: Testing The Waters: Does The Other Side Really Mean That?

Just a little over 20 years ago, I found myself in the middle-east on a business trip. The folks that I was traveling with decided to go down to the bazaar after dinner to see what was available.

While shopping I happened upon an old man who was selling (fake) Rolex's. When I asked him how much one was, he told me US$20.

As I reached into my pocket to pay him, one of my traveling companions stopped me and in a quiet voice said *"He doesn't really mean it, negotiate with him."* It turns out that he was right – I ended up getting the watch for $10. Just in case you are wondering, yes, it does not pay to purchase fakes because that watch stopped working two weeks later.

This same situation often happens during business negotiations. The other side will state that one of their positions such as a firm price or position is non-negotiable.

What do you do now? The last thing that you want to have happen is for the negotiations to end badly. You've got to find out if this is really the case or if they are just saying that as part of their negotiating strategy.

The WRONG thing to do is to charge right at them and offer them a lower price / different position. Instead, what you want to do is to "test" just how firm the other side's position is.

Just because they say that it's immovable, doesn't mean that it really is. Testing means that you need to change the nature of the deal.

Take the "firm" item and add some additional pieces to it. Change the quantities that you are talking about. Change the delivery time: make it longer or shorter.

What you want to do is to mix in items that are not fixed with the ones that are fixed and then go back and negotiate the bottom line. What you may find out is that what was once fixed, is no longer so!

Now this is not the only approach that you can take. Depending on how the negotiations are proceeding, there are four alternative steps that you could take:

1. Try walking out – this may make them chase after you and offer to revisit their "firm" position.

2. Charge on and keep on talking as though you never heard them state that it was a firm position. Note that this approach is extremely dangerous if they call you on it.

3. Protest to a higher power – bring the other side's boss into the negotiation and complain. Once again this can be dangerous if the boss is the one who told them that the point was firm.

4. Finally, reduce the size of the deal being discussed by determining if there are some things that you can do yourself.

Chapter 8

It's Krunch Time!

Chapter 8: It's Krunch Time!

What the heck is a Krunch? In a nutshell, it's a negotiating technique that a buyer can use to squeeze a lower price / better terms out of someone who wants to sell them something.

I've seen this technique used most often when I've been buying a house – it's a classic. I guess that I should confess that I've also used it when I've been selling a house...

How Does It Work?
Here's how the Krunch technique works. The buyer has to have more than one person who wants to sell to them.

When the buyer has collected prices from each of the sellers, then the buyer can go back to every one of them and tell them *"Your price is too high, you can do better."* Generally speaking, each of the sellers ends up lowering their price.

Why Does It Work?
To understand why the simple Krunch technique works so well, you've got to look into the mind of the seller and see what goes on when the buyer tells them that their price is too high:

- Yeah, I built some give into my pricing just in case this happened.
- I knew that what I was selling was too expensive.
- The buyer must have a lower price.
- Hey! The buyer is talking with me so they must like me.
- Oh, oh – does the buyer know something that I don't?

What Are The Drawbacks To Using It?
It doesn't take a rocket scientist to realize that sellers who keep getting Krunch'ed will eventually start to build up defenses to it. Specifically, what you can expect them to do is:

- Boost their prices because they know that they'll be asked to lower them.

- Reduce the quality of the product being offered because they know the price will be lower.

- Drop some services that used to be given.

What Countermeasures Can You Use?
What good is knowing about a negotiating tactic if you don't know how to defend yourself against it? Here are three things that you can do when someone tries the Krunch on you:

- Defend or describe your value. It's not all about price so take some time to tell the buyer about why your offer is better than anyone else's.

- Ask them how much better you have to do. There's no need to lower your price more than they are expecting you to.

- Buy yourself some time by starting to respond by saying *"Hmm..."* This will buy you time and will make the buyer feel obligated to fill the blank space with an explanation as to why they want you to lower your price.

Hopefully you've learned to set your negotiating goals high enough so that you will achieve more than you ever dreamed possible.

Chapter 9

Do You Mind If I "Nibble" On You?

Chapter 9: Do You Mind If I "Nibble" On You?

Ah, the things that they don't teach us in school – like the fine art of nibbling. No, I'm not talking about the process by which you take an hour to eat a cookie by making small bites all around the outside until the whole cookie has been eaten.

Instead, I'm referring to the well-loved negotiating tactic (among others). In the rest of the world, nibbling is a well-accepted business practice by most cultures.

In the U.S. it is generally frowned upon and those who use it are viewed as being cheap. However, it works. It works quite often. Maybe we should find out more...

One of my friends, Mike, is a professional Nibbler. Awhile back I was spending a weekend with him when he decided to go out furniture shopping and so I tagged along.

Mike found a breakfast room table that he really liked. After going back and forth with the sales person, he had finally reached a price that they could both agree on.

Then Mike did something that was unusual. He asked the salesman to throw in the painting that was on the wall in the display area. The surprised salesman thought for a moment, and then agreed.

Mike thanked him and got out his checkbook, paused, and then looking directly at the salesman said *"... and do you think that we could throw in those pillows that are over on that sofa as part of this deal?"* The salesman took a bit longer to answer this time. He said that he could only provide two of the four pillows as a part of the deal. Mike said that that was fine and proceeded to write out his check.

So what had Mike done here? He had gone in to buy a breakfast table and had walked out with a breakfast table, a painting, and two throw pillows.

Truly he was a master Nibbler! The art of nibbling has been around since the dawn of man. The answer to the question of whether or not you should nibble in a given business situation is a matter of your judgment.

Why does Nibbling work? There are five main reasons why the nibble is such an effective negotiating technique:

1. The other side really, really wants to close this deal.

2. The other side has invested a lot of effort to get this far, why blow it now?

3. The "nibble" has a small value in comparison with the value of the whole deal.

4. You are seen as a potential repeat customer if they give in on this one small point.

5. They want you to be left with the feeling that you got a bargain.

Beware the Invisible Nibble! Nibbles can still occur even after a deal is closed. Generally these unseen nibbles are made by buyers who end up paying their bills late, asking for special delivery options or requesting free training that was not part of the original deal.

How Do You Stop The Nibble? So what could have that furniture salesman done to stop my friend Mike from so effectively nibbling on him? Here are a few tips:

- He could have had a published price list. Once Mike saw that he could negotiate the price of the table, everything else was up for grabs.

- He could have insisted that the table was one deal and anything else would have to be another deal.

- He could have said that he didn't have the authority to agree to Mike's nibble request.

- He could have resisted the desire to give in to Mike's requests. If he had been able to hold out just a bit longer, Mike, the nibbler, would have given up.

So now you have another negotiating technique to use. This one will take some guts and the inner strength to give it a try even if you know that you'll be viewed as being cheap. Are you willing to give it a go?

Chapter 10

How Do You Deal With The Rest Of The Iceberg During A Negotiation?

Chapter 10: How Do You Deal With The Rest Of The Iceberg During A Negotiation?

As the captain of the Titanic, Edward John Smith, did a fairly good job of looking out for the parts of icebergs that were above water. What got him in the end is when the Titanic hit a part of an iceberg that he couldn't see because it was below the water. In negotiating, all too often we can fool ourselves into thinking that we know all of the issues that are being negotiated. How wrong we are…

When we negotiate with the other side of the table, the issues that are really being negotiated are often a lot more subtle than those issues that were listed on the agenda at the start of the negotiations. In fact, the issues that originally appeared to be big issues, more often than not turn out to not be all that big of a deal after all.

The things that we often spend the most time talking about, services, goods being sold, and price are of course important. However, the clever negotiator realizes that these are only the tip of the proverbial iceberg.

As a negotiator you need to realize that there will be a large collection of issues that need to be addressed but which will never get written into the final contract. What are these issues you ask?

Simple – they are personal issues that the other side holds dear. Neither side can make these personal demands out loud during the negotiation; however, if you don't address and resolve them, then you won't be reaching an agreement.

If these personal negotiating issues are so important, then what are they so that we can start to look for them? They take many different forms during each negotiation and you are going to have to do some digging to find the ones that relate to your current talks, but here are some examples for you to keep your eyes open for:

- **Personal Schedules**: *"I need to get this negotiation completed by tomorrow because my wife wants to go visit her mother this week."* Both sides of the table have schedules that they need to meet and this can influence the negotiations.

- **Internal Organizational Issues**: *"My boss has been fired and I now work for someone who has a different agenda."* The world is a dynamic place and even as a negotiation goes on, things change. These changes can impact the direction that the negotiation is heading in.

- **Physical Health**: *"I've got a pounding headache."* We need to be constantly reminding ourselves that negotiating has a physical side to it. How either side is currently feeling can have a significant impact on how the negotiations progress.

- **Social Status**: *"I need this negotiation to be successful so that I can show my boss that I'm valuable to the company."* A negotiation does not occur in a bubble – it has visibility and has impacts. Both sides of the table want to be seen in a favorable light when the negotiations are over.

- **Workload**: *"I am already swamped and I need to be careful to not take on any more work."* This is the curse of the modern workplace – too much to do and never enough time to do it. You need to watch the other side to determine if they are dragging their feet because they fear an increase in their workload.

These types of personal issues are a critical part of every negotiation. If you can remain sensitive to these types of issues and are prepared to help the other side find a way to deal with them, then you will be that much closer to successfully concluding the negotiation.

Chapter 11

What If There Was No "What If" Negotiation Tactic?

Chapter 11: What If There Was No "What If" Negotiation Tactic?

During a negotiation, there often arise cases where we'd really like to get the seller to give us information that they really don't want to give to us. If only there was some way to test the other side's willingness to settle with us. Oh, and if there was a way to also "zero in" on the seller's lowest selling price, this would be nice also.

It turns out that such a tactic does exist – it's called (what else) the "**what if**" tactic. An example of how you'd use this tactic would be if you were buying blue widgets from someone.

You'd ask the seller to give you a quote for 100, 1000, 10000, and 20000 blue widgets (sorta like asking "what if I was to buy..."). Once you have a response to your request for bids, you'll have lots of information about their pricing scheme, any setup charges, learning experiences, and production costs.

The "what if" tactic is very powerful when used correctly. In order to help you get the most out of this tactic, here are several suggestions that can help you get information during a negotiation:

1. What if we change the specifications?
2. What if we change when the work is actually done?
3. What if we buy more items than just the ones being negotiated?
4. What if we provide the required materials?
5. What if we increase / decrease the warranty period?
6. What if we increase the quantity?
7. What if we agree to a longer contract?

Now all of these suggestions are great news if you are trying to buy something. But what if you are the one doing the selling? In negotiations, everything is an opportunity.

Once you hear the buyer starting to ask "what if" type questions, you should start to be on alert to what might be coming next. Here are several ways that the seller can react to the "what if" tactic:

- Don't come up with new prices "off the cuff". Take time to plan your prices carefully.

- Realize that not every "what if" question actually needs to be answered. You can avoid answering these types of questions by using responses such as "they won't", "we can't", or "that will be very expensive".

- Use the buyer's deadline to avoid answering a "what if" question. Tell the other side that in order to answer one of their "what if" questions will require more time than they have available to negotiate.

- If you offer a concession, then make it contingent on you receiving their order immediately.

The selling party has a counter tactic called "would you consider" which can be used in response to "what if" questions. Both of these tactics can open new negotiating possibilities that may help both parties move towards a successful solution.

Chapter 12

Negotiation Tactic: The Reverse Auction

Chapter 12: Negotiation Tactic: The Reverse Auction

In the world of negotiations, there are few tactics as old and as well thought of as the "**reverse auction**". This is a powerful negotiating technique that allows a buyer to get the sellers to offer their best pricing for the least amount of work. Not bad if you are a buyer, eh?

Here's how a reverse action works for you if you are a buyer: let's pretend that you wanted to build a house. You go out and get three different offers from three different home builders. As you can imagine, when you get the bids they will contain a confusing mix of different options and time frames.

Your next step will be to call a "reverse auction". You invite all three builders to meet with you. You have them show up early and have them wait in the same room before they meet with you. After they've had a chance to sit and glare at each other for a bit, you then call them in to meet with you one by one.

Each builder will then proceed to tell you why they are the best and why you should avoid selecting the other builders. After you've had a chance to talk with all three builders, you now understand the subtleties and the risks that are involved in building the house that you want.

With all of this new information, you are now able to more clearly refine your specifications because the alternatives have become clear. You can now provide the builders with an updated proposal that they can bid on.

You will end up selecting the builder who can provide the best price while providing the most house for that price. By using a reverse auction, you were able to learn a great deal about building a house and you were able to trade off options that you originally did not know existed.

Why does a reverse auction work for a seller? Simple, there are four reasons:

1. **Competition Works**: when you allow sellers who are competing against each other to "see" each other, it increases the level of competition.

2. **Apply Pressure To Management**: the reverse auction technique allows you to move beyond the salesperson that you are dealing with and actually put pressure on the company's management.

3. **Almost There Syndrome**: each of the sellers has already put a lot of time and effort into responding to your original proposal. This means that they all think that with just a little more effort they can close the deal.

4. **It's Concession Time**: you know that sellers are more averse to losing a deal during negotiations than earlier in a deal. This means that they may make concessions that they normally would not.

This negotiating technique is not without its downside. You need to keep in mind that whichever seller you select is going to feel as though they were put through the ringer. They will probably resent the auction process and will want to make up for being forced to bid a low price.

What this means to you is that any changes that you want to make to the contact after it has been signed will probably end up costing you dearly. Additionally, the seller may end up delivering the product to you late and may even shave some corners on the quality of what gets delivered.

It's from the forge of failure that the steel of success is formed.

Hard Work Does Not Guarantee Success, But Success Does Not Happen Without Hard Work.

- Dr. Jim Anderson

Create An Effective Negotiating Team At Your Company!

Dr. Jim Anderson is available to provide training and coaching on the topics that are the most important to people who have to negotiate: how can my team effectively prepare for and execute a successful negotiation that will get us what we both want and need?

Dr. Anderson believes that in order to both learn and remember what he says, audiences need to laugh. Each one of his speeches is full of fun and humor so that what he says "sticks" with everyone.

Dr. Anderson's Negotiating Training Includes:

1. How to plan for a negotiation: what information do you need and where can you find it?

2. What's the best way to explore how a deal can be created during a negotiation?

3. How can you bring a negotiation to a close without giving in to the other side?

Dr. Jim Anderson works with over 100 customers per year. To invite Dr. Anderson to work with you, contact him at:

Phone: 813-418-6970 or
Email: jim@BlueElephantConsulting.com

Photo Credits:

Cover - By: Rob Young
http://www.flickr.com/photos/rob-young/

Chapter 1 - By: deb
http://www.flickr.com/photos/slidingsideways/

Chapter 2 - By: Burns Library, Boston College
http://www.flickr.com/photos/bc-burnslibrary/

Chapter 3 - By: Koon
http://www.flickr.com/photos/koonisutra/

Chapter 4 - By: Nicole Lee
http://www.flickr.com/photos/nicolelee/

Chapter 5 - By: World Trade Organization
http://www.flickr.com/photos/world_trade_organization/

Chapter 6 - By: Greg Bishop
http://www.flickr.com/photos/konabish/

Chapter 7 - By: Brian Uhreen
http://www.flickr.com/photos/snype451/

Chapter 8 - By: KMar Tsai
http://www.flickr.com/photos/kmar/

Chapter 9 - By: Ludie Cochrane
http://www.flickr.com/photos/ludiecochrane/

Chapter 10 - By: Marie and Alistair Knock
http://www.flickr.com/photos/aknock/

Chapter 11 - By: Damián Navas
http://www.flickr.com/photos/wingedwolf/

Chapter 12 - By: Juan Alberto Puentes Puertas
http://www.flickr.com/photos/japp1967/

Other Books By The Author

Product Management

- Product Development Lessons For Product Managers: How Product Managers Can Create Successful Products

- Customer Lessons For Product Managers: Techniques For Product Managers To Better Understand What Their Customers Really Want

- Product Failure Lessons For Product Managers: Examples Of Products That Have Failed For Product Managers To Learn From

- Communication Skills For Product Managers: The Communication Skills That Product Managers Need To Know How To Use In Order To Have A Successful Product

- How To Have A Successful Product Manager Career: The Things That You Need To Be Doing TODAY In Order To Have A Successful Product Manager Career

- Product Manager Product Success: How to keep your product on track and make it become a success

Public Speaking

- How To Give A Great Presentation: Presentation techniques that will transform a speech into a memorable event

- How To Rehearse In Order To Give The Perfect Speech: How to effectively rehearse your next speech to that your message be remembered forever!

- Secrets To Creating The Perfect Speech: How to create a speech that will make your message be remembered forever!

- Secrets To Organizing The Perfect Speech: How to organize the best speech of your life!

- Secrets To Planning The Perfect Speech: How to plan to give the best speech of your life

CIO Skills

- Critical CIO Management Skills: Decision Making Skills That Every CIO Needs To Have In Order To Be Able To Make The Right Choices

- How CIOs Can Make Innovation Happen: Tips And Techniques For CIOs To Use In Order To Make Innovation Happen In Their IT Department

- CIO Communication Skills Secrets: Tips And Techniques For CIOs To Use In Order To Become Better Communicators

- Managing Your CIO Career: Steps That CIOs Have To Take In Order To Have A Long And Successful Career

- CIO Business Skills: How CIOs can work effectively with the rest of the company!

IT Manager Skills

- Staffing Skills IT Managers Must Have: Tips And Techniques That IT Managers Can Use In Order To Correctly Staff Their Teams

- Secrets Of Effective Leadership For IT Managers: Tips And Techniques That IT Managers Can Use In Order To Develop Leadership Skills

- IT Manager Career Secrets: Tips And Techniques That IT Managers Can Use In Order To Have A Successful Career

- IT Manager Budgeting Skills: How IT Managers Can Request, Manage, Use, And Track Their Funding

Negotiating

- Learn How To Argue In Your Next Negotiation: How To Develop The Skill Of Effective Arguing In A Negotiation In Order To Get The Best Possible Outcome

- How To Open Your Next Negotiation: How To Start A Negotiation In Order To Get The Best Possible Outcome

- Preparing For Your Next Negotiation: What You Need To Do BEFORE A Negotiation Starts In Order To Get The Best Possible Deal

Miscellaneous

- Power Distribution Unit (PDU) Secrets: What Everyone Who Works In A Data Center Needs To Know!

- Making The Jump: How To Land Your Dream Job When You Get Out Of College!

How To Develop The Skill Of Exploring What Is Possible In A Negotiation In Order To Reach The Best Possible Deal

This book has been written with one goal in mind – to show you how to use the skill of exploring in your next negotiation. It's not easy being a negotiator and so we're going to show you how to get the information that you need in order to get the deal that you want!

Let's Make Your Negotiation A Success!

What You'll Find Inside:

- **GOT TO KEEP 'EM SEPARATED — ROLES IN NEGOTIATING**

- **YOU WANT A BARGAIN? LEARN HOW OTHER CULTURES BARTER**

- **FUNNY MONEY AIN'T SO FUNNY WHEN IT'S YOUR MONEY**

- **TESTING THE WATERS: DOES THE OTHER SIDE REALLY MEAN THAT?**

Dr. Jim Anderson brings his 25 years of real-world experience to this book. He's been a negotiator at some of the world's largest firms. He's going to show you what you need to do (and not do!) in order to get the best deal out of your next negotiation!

www.ingramcontent.com/pod-product-compliance
Lightning Source LLC
Chambersburg PA
CBHW071814170526
45167CB00003B/1306